40-No More Excuses

Myths The Over 40 Crowd Believe!

Dating After 40-No More Excuses
Myths The Over 40 Crowd Believe!

Cover Art: Rich Tamayo, TVP Studios
Photography - Scott Aguilar
Model - Stephanie Sheppard

www.GettingWhatYouWant.com

Getting What You Want Publishing
1230 Crescent Dr, Glendale, CA 91205

Dating After 40
No More Excuses

Myths The
Over 40 Crowd
Believe!

**Purpose: To Awaken Women To The
Power They Already Have And To
Get Exactly What They Want In
Every Facet Of Their Life.**

Susan Sheppard

Table of Contents

Chapter 1:

The Only Places To Meet Men Are Bars!

Nothing could be farther from the truth. Men are everywhere. Some of the best places to meet men are seminars, adult education classes, participating in sports, going to work.

Open your eyes. Look for men you have never considered before. It is really important to widen your comfort zone. Yes, you can meet a man in a bar but for women over 40 it is not a likely place to look. The magic key to meeting someone is to take action. Participate in something you have an interest in doing. Go to church and church activities. Take dancing lessons. Take a computer class. Take a leave of absence from your job and take a traveling job. Go to a Real estate conference or some conference where the ratio is 10:1 men to women.

Check out www.MeetUp.com and search for activities that interest you. Then participate. Join an organization that requires you to attend meetings, classes or social events. The idea in joining an organization is to expand your horizons, not to meet others of the same sex who are having the same issues that you are. So be adventurous and join something that you know nothing about that is heavily populated by the opposite sex. That is how you meet people of the opposite sex. Then go to their gatherings and ask a lot of questions. Be truly interested in what is going on.

Additionally, it isn't necessary to spend money to go to conferences. Look around, pay attention. There are free seminars all over the place. No matter what age you are or where your interests lie, you can find introductory seminars on almost any subject on the Internet or in your local paper.

Finally do not overlook meeting members of the opposite sex by utilizing online dating services or personal ads in the local papers. Some of my clients have met and married fine, upstanding, wonderful human beings in these ways. Take it upon yourself to expand your consciousness about who the opposite sex is for you and then practice, practice, practice expanding your horizons.

If you want a man, you have to do the work. There are many women who are totally unwilling to do

what it takes to get what they
want and that includes a man. So,
be the exception and that will
even the odds.
Action is required.

Chapter 2:

All The Good Men Are Taken!

Without dispute, the numbers are different when you are over 40 than when you were 18. However, from the perspective of someone over 40, though the availability of 18 year olds is much more evident, what you get in the 18-25 age group is an undeveloped, immature, financially unstable child. When you are 40+, you are interested in meeting a good man.

What constitutes a good man? The essential qualities of a good man are a respect for women, a productive human being who can support himself and it would be a bonus if he could support a family too, an intelligent man who participates in his own life, honesty, a healthy sexual appetite and the ability to perform, vitality and health, an excitement about life, an interesting man who is interested in world events and open to new ideas. A good man to me is one to whom I am attracted for who he is. By the way, though it is important for an attraction to exist, it is not physical attractiveness that is most important. Don't start your requirement list with tall, dark and handsome or you will surely be disappointed with real men.

There are plenty of these kinds of men available. It is necessary to do some work to uncover them, but they do exist. Some have baggage, but some are just shy. There are plenty of men over 35 who want to be in relationship with a woman. Some even are anxious to have a family.

Most do not have a clue how to go about making that happen. It is a woman's responsibility to choose a man and condition him to be a good man in relationship. Men do not inherently know how to do that. Any man that you perceive to be a good man that is already taken has been indoctrinated into the "good man society" by a woman. That woman could have been his mother, a girlfriend, a wife, a boss or some woman who took the time to teach him how to treat a woman. It is a woman's responsibility to teach a man her standards. In other words, find a man who has the basic qualities of a good man and customize him with love.

Please note this does not mean that you can change him. You cannot find a man who has a serious character defect and expect to convert him to a good man. It is important that you as a woman do not settle for less than what you want from a man.

Without being a demanding unreasonable bitch, you can get a man who loves you, to treat you with respect and fulfill your needs. You will however, be expected to treat him with respect and satisfy his needs as well. That is included in the definition of a relationship. The essential ingredients in a romantic relationship include chemistry, love with respect and compatibility. Without all three,

your odds of success are severely
diminished.
Take action.

Chapter 3:
Women Over 40
Hate Sex!

There are some women over 40 who don't like sex, but the majority of women in general do like sex, good sex. What they do not like is mediocre, expected, duty sex that allows the man to get satisfied and leaves them frustrated and unsatisfied. I am going to offer an opinion here that might be very unpopular, however, I believe that it is true.

Women settle for bad sex because they do not feel secure enough in their own attractiveness to ask for good sex. Neither men nor women know what sex is all about when they start having it. They just

follow their instincts and respond
to their hormones and sexual
instincts. How many "mandatory"
courses in sexual satisfaction have
been offered to adults? We don't
see those offered frequently.

Women don't like bad sex. Men
believe that they are good lovers
because they have been lied to by
women who have been afraid to
teach their men how to make love
to them in a way that provides
them with sexual satisfaction.
Women are afraid of offending a
man they are sexing because it is a
common belief that men have
fragile egos especially when it

comes to their sexual proficiency. Women also have guilt feelings about what it takes to bring them to orgasm. They are embarrassed about the fact that a woman requires foreplay and sexual stimulation in order to achieve arousal and the ability to climax.

All of the above is the justification for women faking orgasm. It is so easy for a man to climax and it is more complicated for a woman to climax. So what! Isn't that what relationship is all about. Delving into intimate secrets and each other's vulnerability makes sexual satisfaction all the more delicious. Relationship gives each party permission to ask the unmentionable questions and be naked and vulnerable for pleasure. Men are turned on by women who enjoy being naked, playful and sensuous with them.

What I mean by a woman's attractiveness is not just her physical beauty, but also her sense of self---assuredness and confidence in her power as a sexual being to capture her lover's attention for the extended amount of time that it takes for her to get aroused and come to climax.

FACT: It takes a woman longer (on the average) to become sexually aroused and reach orgasm than it takes for a man to achieve the same. Ultimately, what is more true is that women over 40 don't tolerate bad sex and don't have the energy or the desire to retrain men who think they are great lovers to be responsive, attentive lovers.

Does this absolve men from any responsibility in this sexual equation? Absolutely not, a man needs to be cognizant of what it takes for his woman to achieve sexual satisfaction and do whatever it takes to take her there. Take action and own your sexual pleasure.

Chapter 4:
Women Want A
Sugar Daddy!

This one is a myth that many men accept as truth. Women are quite capable of taking care of themselves and more often than not they take care of everyone around them as well. Look at the numbers of single parents who are women. Recognize that many women have left men because the men have expected them to take care of them too. Women take care of children; women with male siblings usually are expected to take care of aging parents. So if women are capable of taking care of everyone, why do they want a man to take care of them? Women are tired of doing it alone. They want a partner, someone to share the burden. They want someone who can regenerate them and recharge them. They want a man to love and cherish them and simply lighten the load a little.

The women that I have encountered who are looking for a relationship are not looking for someone to completely relieve them of their financial burdens so they can sit home and watch soap operas and eat bonbons.

Speaking for myself, I would like someone to meet me at home when I arrive. I'd like someone to help carry in the groceries, and help cook and eat the meals. I wouldn't give up working. Working is what I do. I like feeling productive, making a contribution and earning my own money. I wouldn't give that up. What I want is someone to hug me, kiss me, make love to me, listen to me and play with me. All of these things recharge me and make me able to go out into the world and make a difference.

Is it different for men? I don't think so. I believe that men feel battered by the outside world as well. They possibly are not as

29

verbal about seeking to be recharged. Some men are willing to settle for a beer, their left hand and the remote control on their TV to keep them going.

Women seeking relationship want a partner who will provide affection, understanding, intimacy and someone who will talk and listen to them. Contrary to popular opinion they are not seeking money, protection and total financial support. So we have to look at a lot of frogs before we find a good man so when you actually find one, do whatever it takes to make it work.

Women don't need a man to survive. If a woman is looking to be in a relationship it is because she has decided that she wants a relationship. She wants someone to play with her. She wants a little fun and pleasure in her life. She doesn't want a daddy or another child, she wants a real man who wants to play house and have some fun.

Take action.

Chapter 5:
Women Expect
Too Much!

I do believe that men are capable of much more than they would like to have us believe. I have witnessed men who step up to the challenge of producing results even when they did not believe that it was possible. The real challenge is for the women in these relationships to put forth their desires in a way that their man can hear them.

Additionally it is always inspiring for a woman to ask a man for more than he thinks he can produce, if and only if she absolutely believes in him. A man will produce for the woman he loves to the level of her expectations. So if your expectations are low and you don't express them with acknowledgement of his ability, you won't get what you want. I know this sounds way too simple, but it really works.

Men want to please women. Especially, a man wants to please the woman he loves. The obstacle is they never know what will please her. On a daily basis, I witness various men jumping through hoops and overextending themselves to please a woman and then watching while the woman reams him because he didn't do whatever it was she wanted, the way she wanted it done.

For this miscarriage of justice, I blame the both the women and the men. How can I be such a traitor to other women? Simple. Women do not ask directly for what they want. They hint, or give convoluted requests (Women at fault) and men simply do not respond appropriately.

Because they are men, they do not ask for clarification. (Men at fault) They presume to know what the woman is requesting. Then they

work real hard to produce a result
that isn't even close to what the
woman wanted. Women then get
angry because they think the men
are sabotaging the relationship
and deliberately creating the
wrong results.

Men just get confused because
they have expended a whole lot of
energy producing a wrong result.
When women learn how to
effectively ask for what they want,
men produce amazing results. My
interpretation of the myth that
women expect too much is that
women don't expect nearly
enough. They stop asking and

36

continually lower their
expectations because they don't
initially get their desired results
and then men just stop trying to
please the women. Then
everything in the relationship goes
to the dogs and there is serious
work to reclaim the Love!
Take action.

Chapter 6:

The M Word (Marriage) Will Spur The Great Escape!

It is possible if you declare your intentions right away, i.e. I am looking for a committed relationship and I want to get married, that you will scare some men away. However, if you can scare them away with that at the beginning of a relationship, it is likely that you could scare them away after you have been in it for a while. In other words if that could scare a man away, he wasn't what you wanted in the first place.

What you are looking for is a man who wants to be in a committed relationship. You want to find someone who says; hey that is what I am looking for as well. You can chase those guys who run all over the place, you are not going to change them.

Don't think that you can make a man change his mind about marrying and having kids because you are so wonderful. Your wonderfulness has very little to do with what a man intends to do with his life. If you do manage to get him to commit to marriage, it is likely that he will find another way to run away if he so desires.

The truth of it is that when you are over 40, you just don't have time to play hide and seek with a man. The "I wonder what he thinks of me" routine belongs to teenagers. You are now playing an adult version of the dating game. What that entails is honesty. If you haven't figured out by now that relationship is an intense experience and requires complete openness and vulnerability in order to succeed, you are not ready for an adult relationship. So give up your illusions of playing seductive, manipulative games and confront the situation head on. Women do the choosing and women do the ending of relationships so why not be straight about it? Weed out the guys who are not serious about settling down and don't worry about the ones who run when they hear the word marriage or commitment or relationship. They wouldn't make good partners anyway.

Look for a man with whom you are compatible in all your deal breaker areas and with whom you share great chemistry and true love with respect.

Trust me, they really do exist.
You just have to set your bar high
and keep expanding your comfort
zone. They usually are not where
you expect them to be.
Take action.

Chapter 7:

Men And Commitment Are Like Oil And Water!

Who are men really? Men are creatures of impulse. They are sensitive human beings who once were little boys. They have feelings that they don't exhibit because they were taught to stifle them. They want to be loved and appreciated for the good things they do. They really try to please women but most of them don't have a clue how to go about it. They are poor in the communication department. They are strong in the silent department. They usually have a passion that they don't always advertise. They like having respect and adoration. They don't call unless they have

something to say. They do not
think about how to have a
relationship, they just want one.
They do not want to have to
dissect and analyze their
relationship; they just want it to
be there.

They do have mid-life crises
where they go a little crazy and
think that life has passed them by
and it may take a while for them
to regain their sanity. They love to
look at pretty women. Most will
stray if they don't get enough sex
at home, don't feel appreciated at
home, or if sex is offered and no
one will ever know. They do not

want to repeat themselves. If they say they love you once, that should be enough. They do not read minds. They are obtuse about hints. They buy presents that they would like to have themselves.

Good men respect women. They admire the physical ability of women to bear and nurse children. They want to be heroes. They have large egos and hate to be wrong. They especially hate it when they do something stupid and get caught. They still do stupid things. So what does all of this have to do with their ability to commit? They don't want to make a mistake and the way to avoid a mistake is to do nothing at all. If the status quo is okay why change it. It is only when they experience discomfort that they will be motivated to commit.

What causes discomfort? Fear. Fear of loss. Fear of making a mistake. Fear of change. Fear of not getting what they want. Fear of settling for less than the best. I think that most of them will commit if the right woman chooses them at the right time. Take action.

Chapter 8:
Plastic Surgery
Is The Answer!

A woman who thinks she needs plastic surgery, to get or hold on to a man, has absolutely no knowledge of what men really want, or she chooses abusive men. That is not to say that plastic surgery is never indicated. People who have physical traits that seriously detract from the ability of that person to interact with the opposite sex should have surgery.

It is the beautiful people who believe that plastic surgery will find them a man or keep a failing relationship from deteriorating that I question. The truth is real men notice far less about women's appearance than other women do. Real men think women are beautiful in all sizes and shapes. Men are very visual and always appreciate beauty but for the most part they are blind to the defects that women believe make them totally unattractive.

Let me tell you a little story. Once upon a time I met a man at a hotel in Palm Springs for a weekend. Through miscommunication I arrived earlier than expected and he informed me that a stripper was arriving for one of the guy's birthday. He invited me to watch expecting me to say no, but I wanted to be there.

It was a revelation to me. I watched a young girl with a bad complexion, no makeup, stringy hair and a lumpy body with sagging breasts and stretch marks strip naked and dance totally unashamed for a room full of 20 guys and me. The reality was that she was very wary and suspicious of me and totally comfortable with the men. All of the men were turned on and appreciative of her performance. I went through an experience of "this does not compute". I could not understand how these guys could be turned on by such (to me) an unattractive girl. What I discovered in this experience was that it was her uninhibitedness, her attitude and her willingness to be and play naked in front of them that was such a turn on. The men did not notice her complexion, her hair, her stretch marks or her lumpiness. What they noticed was her sexiness, her nakedness and her willingness to engage them. It was a truly enlightening experience for me.

After that experience I began to notice that many husbands don't even notice when their wives gain weight. They have a picture in their mind of the woman they fell in love with and that is what they see when their wife is naked.

Not to say that a woman can't get sloppy and disregard her looks completely, but those women who think they need plastic surgery to compete are trying to be someone they are not. They are fighting their age instead of embracing it.

They are in denial about what men really are interested in having in a woman. They are inauthentic.

If a man rejects a woman for strictly her appearance, he does not to deserve to have her.

Take action.

Chapter 9: Women Seriously Outnumber Men Over 40!

So What? There are also more women over 40 who are not interested in having a relationship. There are women who are only interested in children, career, or other women. If you want a man, you can have a man. You merely have to decide that is what you want. I am so convinced that this is true, that I have written a book about it.

My book, "How to Get What You Want from Your Man Anytime" has a chapter devoted to dating and expanding your boundaries and expectations. In that chapter there is a specific strategy for

finding the man of your dreams.
Get clarity about who you are
looking for.

Decide on the values, the beliefs,
the intentions, the deal breakers,
and the compatibility that you
desire and write it down. Then go
start meeting a lot of men until
you raise your self-esteem to the
level that attracts the man you
want.

Do not be concerned about the
scarcity of men. That is truly the
myth. There are so many men out
there who would love to be in a
relationship. They just don't have

a clue how to go about starting. If
you believe, you can achieve.

Once I wanted to buy a house. At
least 20 realtors told me there was
no way I could qualify. I kept
looking because I knew I could
have what I wanted. It took a
while but I finally found a realtor
who said I will help you and I
agree you could buy a house. I
also had about 20 criteria and
wasn't willing to settle for less
than what I wanted. After many
months of searching, I found the
perfect house, in the perfect
location for the perfect price. My
intention was so strong that at

closing when escrow asked for
$5000.00 more than I had been
promised I would need. A
coworker happened to have
exactly that amount in her pocket
that day. She had just taken it
from her IRA for her contractor.
She didn't have to pay him for
another week. She handed it to me
in order to close escrow that same
day. I was able to return the
money to her a week later. It was
a magical experience and I know
that it is possible for all of us to
create those kinds of miracles.

On my wall is this quote: "The
first step to getting what you want

out of life is this: Decide what you want! If you know what you want, you're going to get it. Nothing's going to stop you from fulfilling your dreams and desires. Just remember not everything is going to go exactly as planned.

Just when the caterpillar thought the world was over, it became a butterfly"

The other fact I want you to consider is this. What would happen if you would consider a relationship with a younger man? Many of the truths that are stated in the next myth about younger

women and older men are
absolutely true about older women
and younger men. Women my age
are looking almost exclusively at
younger men because the men my
age on the whole are boring,
stodgy, unimaginative, cynical
and chauvinistic not to mention
suffering from ED.

There are exceptions to the above,
but it involves an effort to search
and meet a lot of frogs before you
find your prince.

There are only a certain number of
men who can sustain a
relationship with an older woman

who is adventurous, filled with vitality, possibility thinking towards the future, physical health and stamina, a lack of cynicism and absence of baggage, including victim mentality and drama. So, You, be that woman and of course, you must choose wisely.

Grabbing the first one who shows an interest is not the idea. Maintaining the unwillingness to settle for less than what you want is still your primary focus. Just don't exclude men who are younger, just because of the age difference. Age is just a number. Take action.

Chapter 10 :

Men Are Only Interested In Women Half Their Age!

This could be categorized as every man's fantasy. However, the truth of the matter is that only a fraction of one percent of the men out there are able to attract and hold onto a woman 15-20 years younger than themselves.

The fault lies equally on the men and the women. The common accepted belief is that the younger women are bimbos, beautiful, sexy and stupid and the older men are rich and looking for arm candy. In the honest relationships that exist in these parameters the truth is nothing like that. The themes that repeat themselves

over and over again are surprising
in that rarely were beauty and
youth the deciding factors for
these extraordinary men.

Among their reasons, the men
cited adventurousness, vitality,
possibility thinking towards the
future, physical health and
stamina, a lack of cynicism and
absence of baggage, including
victim mentality and drama. They
found the younger women to be
less egocentric and narcissistic,
while the women over 40 related
everything that happens in the
world to their own circumstances.

Many were bitter, negative and hopeless.

There is no denying that men are visual and attracted to beautiful, young, nubile, voluptuous women. The truth is they enjoy the view. They like to look, but most men that I know who are over 40 who have attempted relationships with women 10-20 years younger than themselves, have been very disillusioned by their experience.

One told me the sex was great at first, but after two weeks of nothing but sex, he was exhausted. He existed in this relationship for almost two years and when it was over, he confessed that he was very relieved to be rid of the "psycho bitch" that had been ruining his life for the past two years. The girl was 23 and he was 46 when they met. His oldest son was 20. The young woman was not capable of adapting and handling the level of maturity it took to be a stepmother to his children. She wanted to party and live the life of a twenty-something. Although they had chemistry, their compatibility stopped with that. They both stuck it out for two years because they had made some major commitments and the children were involved. He told me later it was like having another kid. He eventually bought her a car and sent her back home to the East Coast. He is now involved with a woman who is in her early 40's and he tells me that he couldn't be happier. He says she is intelligent, capable, beautiful, and sexy and she loves being with him and his children.

Another 40+ never-married man that I coached, was interested in having a relationship with a younger woman for very specific reasons. He wanted to get married and have children and he was concerned with the ability of 40+ women to have the capacity and the desire to start a family.

Modern medicine makes it possible for women to bear children into their 50's if they so desire. Desire is the key word here. Many women over 40 are too used up to want children. That is part of the adventurousness, vitality and possibility thinking that the older men referenced when they were surveyed about younger women. This man encountered many of the same issues that the other man did with his younger girlfriend. She wanted to party and he was pretty much over the party scene. He wanted her to have a career until they had children. She wanted to stay home and keep house and wasn't sure she wanted to have children with him.

This relationship ended because she refused to grow up. The upshot of this discussion is that women over 40 can learn a lot from their younger counterparts. Their primary focus has to be attitude. Possibility thinking and focus are crucial ingredients. The bottom line is that vitality and aliveness along with authenticity, honesty and vulnerability all contribute to finding and keeping a hot relationship. The most important reality of all when it comes to having a relationship is that you must decide that you want one. Then Take action.

The end result is myths are myths and we can disregard them if we choose.

Chapter 11:

What To Do Now!

If you have read this far, you must be interested in moving forward, so I want to talk about what might be your next step. First I want you to seriously ponder what has stopped you from pursuing a relationship up to now. I know that might be any of a million reasons but each one of you has justification for what has stopped or defeated or stalled you up to now. If your reason is not obvious to you right now, take some time and write about it.

The best way to get good answers from your other than conscious mind is to ask yourself a question just before you fall asleep and in the morning some answers will pop into your head.

It might sound a little "woo woo" if you have never done this kind of work, but it actually works. Try it.

Next step is to acknowledge that whatever has stopped or stalled you is associated with some level of fear and it's best to acknowledge that fear and be appreciative that your mind is taking care of you in that way. Then, finally, set aside the fear and decide that you are going to stretch and expand your comfort zone a little. And I do mean a little. Take baby steps. Have a conversation with someone of the opposite sex that you normally would avoid. Even better, you initiate the conversation. Talk about something innocent, like the weather or something that you have observed. Just do it. Your confidence and self---esteem will automatically increase a little bit. Then do it again. Don't worry about what that person will think of you, it is irrelevant.

You are doing research and working on growing your self-esteem and comfort zone. It is a slow process but it really is necessary for you to start healing where you are.

Love with CLASS coaching is a System developed 25 years ago to heal wounded or broken hearts from relationship disasters. If you want love in your life but don't know what to do next….
Get the Complete Love With CLASS System

http://bit.ly/2rd2zVf

We can change your belief and grow your self esteem so that you absolutely have no doubt about what will happen for you. Join the Love with CLASS Movement and brush away your fears, get a plan and take action so you can get what you want NOW!

Susan Sheppard
www.GettingWhatYouWant.com